NOOMA Group® | Collection 002 Discussion Guide
Copyright © 2010 by Flannel, P.O. Box 3228, Grand Rapids, MI 49501-3228, USA.

Published by Zondervan, 5300 Patterson Avenue SE, Grand Rapids, MI 49530, USA.

——

ISBN 978-0-310-32541-3

Published in association with Yates & Yates, www.yates2.com.

——

Printed in the United States of America

09 10 11 12 13 14 15 • 10 9 8 7 6 5 4 3 2 1

NOOMA Group® | Collection 002 Discussion Guide

—

Contents

Foreword

Jesus lived with the awareness that God is doing something, right here, right now, and anybody can be a part of it. He encouraged his listeners to search, to question, to wrestle with the implications of what he was saying and doing. He inspired, challenged, provoked, comforted, and invited people to be open to God's work in this world. Wherever he went, whatever he did, Jesus started discussions about what matters most, because for Jesus, God is always inviting us to open our eyes and join in.

NOOMA is a series of short films that explore our world from a perspective of Jesus.

NOOMA is an invitation to search, question, and join the discussion.

NOOMA films don't claim to hold all the answers, but they do claim to start the conversation.

Introduction

—

This Collection 002 Discussion Guide is designed to accompany NOOMA Group Collection 002 and is intended to facilitate discussions based on the themes and questions raised in Collection 002 Films. The Collection 002 Discussion Guide helps viewers delve more deeply and meaningfully into the issues raised in Collection 002 Films — 005 Noise, 006 Kickball, 007 Luggage, and 008 Dust. Viewers will explore and discuss issues such as why we are so afraid of silence, why we don't always get what we want if God is such a loving God, why forgiveness is so difficult, and what exactly God sees in us. Watch the films with friends, open the book, and together begin to search, question, and join the discussion.

How to Use This Book

Get a group of friends together ... not too many that nobody gets to talk, and not too few that you can't get a decent conversation started. Get a load of whatever everybody likes to eat and drink, hand out the discussion guides, make sure everybody's got a pen, and start the first film.

Each film lasts about 10 minutes ... they're short ... but they pack a lot in. You can follow along with the guide ... we made it easy by including a few quotes from the films to help you keep your place. After each quote, you might see a question ... or two, or maybe more ... questions aimed at provoking thought ... introspection. Take notes. Draw pictures. Do anything you need, or want. Just save your comments for later.

At the end of each film, dive into the discussion questions. You can discuss the questions asked after the quotes, or you can go straight to the others at the end of the section, the ones labeled "Go a Little Deeper." Just remember, though, the discussion is the important thing — not the questions. The questions are meant as guidelines — nothing more.

Then again, if things start to go a little off tangent, bring it back in if you want by moving on to the next question. If you're fine with the direction things are going, let it go. The point isn't to make sure you solve the world's problems in your discussion of the films.

The point is to ask questions, and to start looking at those questions from what might be a different perspective, one that considers Jesus and what he is doing in the world.

At the end of the discussion question section on each film there is an application, called "Before Moving On." It might be something you all do as a group. It might be something each person is expected to do in the coming days on their own. It might be both. Whatever it is, challenge each other to do it. Hold each other accountable.

After the application, you'll find a couple or more questions titled "Further Personal Reflection." Do these in your car on the way home … or in bed at night … in the shower … wherever … just spend some time wrestling with them.

Go at whatever pace everyone is comfortable. There are a lot of questions here. We don't recommend a 24-hour marathon, but we also don't recommend you try to cram four films in a two-hour session — take your time, let the discussions evolve, and try to let them last as long as they need to last. Don't feel like you have to get to all the questions or that you have to do the questions in order.

Make sure everyone has a Bible. And make sure you open it, and read it, and don't be afraid to disagree with what is said, or what others say. Look for yourself what the Bible says. Check out its claims about who Jesus is, and what he's doing in the world. Ultimately this isn't about a film, or a deep discussion … or any of that, really. Ultimately, it's about you and what you do with this Jesus. Is he who he says he is, or is he not?

Take some time to pray at the beginning — ask God to open your hearts and minds to what he would have you learn. Take some more time to pray again at the end — for each other, and for God's Word to further penetrate your hearts in the days ahead.

Always keep in mind, NOOMA films don't claim to have all the answers … but they do claim to start the conversation.

Enjoy.

Noise | 005
—

Why are we so afraid of silence?

Noise | 005

—

Be still, and know that I am God.

—

Psalm 46:10

Why is silence so hard to deal with? Why is it so much easier for us to live our lives with a lot of things going on all the time than to just be in silence? We're constantly surrounded with "voices" that are influencing us on how to think, feel, and behave. Movies, music, TV, Internet, cell phones, and a never-ending barrage of advertising. There's always something going on. Always noise in our lives. But maybe there's a connection between the amount of noise in our lives and our inability to hear God. If God sometimes feels distant from us, maybe it's not because he's not talking to us, but simply because we aren't really listening.

In this film, we discuss the noise that invades and pervades our lives every day. We talk about how the world is getting more and more noisy and that, as a result, it's becoming more and more difficult to find peace and quiet in it. We relate the story of Elijah, the Jewish prophet, who was told to go up on the mountain, where God was going to show up. Elijah withstood a great wind, an earthquake, and fire, until he finally heard God's voice in the quiet. Noise | 005 challenges us to look at our own lives and question whether or not we are so surrounded by noise, both audible and visual, that we cannot hear God.

If anything strikes you while you watch Noise | 005, write it down … or make a note and finish it later … whatever comes to your mind … just get it on paper … and then when the time comes, talk about it …

Talk about Noise | 005

"I was reading about this guy named Bernie Krause who records nature sounds for film and television. And he was saying that in 1968, in order to get one hour of undisturbed natural sound, like no airplanes, no cars, it would take him about 15 hours of recording time."

1. Does Bernie Krause's comment surprise you?

"And he was saying that today, in order to get that same one hour of undisturbed sound, it takes him two thousand hours of recording time."

2. Is your world loud?

The LORD said, "Go out and stand on the mountain in the presence of the LORD, for the LORD is about to pass by." Then a great and powerful wind tore the mountains apart and shattered the rocks before the LORD, but the LORD was not in the wind. After the wind there was an earthquake, but the LORD was not in the earthquake. After the earthquake came a fire, but the LORD was not in the fire. And after the fire came a gentle whisper. When Elijah heard it, he pulled his cloak over his face and went out and stood at the mouth of the cave. Then a voice said to him, "What are you doing here, Elijah?"

---

1 Kings 19:11–13

3. Do you expect God's voice to be spectacular?

"And then comes the still, small voice of God. Now, there's all this discussion about what exactly this voice is."

4. Can you hear God's voice?

"So some translators translate the phrase that God was in the sound of sheer silence."

5. Does silence make a sound?

"God wasn't in the wind. God wasn't in the earthquake. God wasn't in the fire. God was in the silence."

6. Do you sense God's presence in your silent moments?

"One-hundred and eighty-three million people are regularly exposed to noise levels labeled as excessive by the Environmental Protection Agency."

7. Is the noise in your life excessive?

"Do you have a cell phone? A pager? Voice-mail? Do you have a cell phone with voice-mail and e-mail?"

8. How many ways can people get in touch with you?

9. Is that enough?

"Do you have a TV? More than one TV?"

10. Are you afraid of missing something?

"Do you have a radio on all day? On at work, in the car, at home?"

11. What are you afraid of missing?

"Is there such a thing as visual noise? Do you wish there were more billboards along the roads you drive? Do we have enough strip malls yet?"

"Do you feel like God is distant? Do you wish God's voice would be louder in your life?"

12. Whose voice is loudest in your life?

"Is there a connection between the amount of noise in our lives and our inability to hear God?"

"You can buy wired clothing now. Coats and jackets equipped with cell phones and MP3 players."

13. Do you welcome the latest gadgets to keep you entertained?

But Jesus often withdrew to lonely places and prayed.

—

Luke 5:16

"These were regular disciplines Jesus had. Silence. Solitude."

"When was the last time you were in a solitary place?"

"Why is it easier to surround myself with noise and keep moving than to stop, be silent, and listen?"

"Maybe the healing and guidance we desperately need is not going to come from one more meeting or therapy session or sermon or self-help book but from simply listening for the voice of God."

"Is it possible that you have been searching for God in the winds, the earthquakes, and fires, and he is waiting to speak to you in the silence?"

14. Have you been searching for God in the wrong places?

15. Are you listening for God, or have you given up even trying?

Noise | 005 is finished. Now it's your turn. Go back, reread some of the quotes from the film, and discuss the questions raised by those quotes. Then, when you're ready, if there's time, move on to the following questions for more in-depth discussion.

Go a Little Deeper

1. Did the several minutes of silence in the film make you uneasy? Was it awkward in any way? Why or why not?

2. Think of your typical day. Think of the numerous sources of noise in your life. Name some of the noises you deal every day. Are you comfortable with your noise? Why or why not?

3. Why is silence so hard for some people to deal with? What about you? Is silence difficult for you to deal with? Why or why not?

4. What does the quote from Bernie Krause say about our world? Would you consider that progress? Why or why not?

5. Reread the statistic from the Environmental Protection Agency. Do you believe too much noise can be dangerous to you physically? How? Do you believe too much noise can be dangerous to you mentally? How? Emotionally? How?

6. Do you believe too much noise can be dangerous to you spiritually? How?

7. When you're with another person, do you find it easier to talk or to listen? Why?

8. When you're with a group of people, do you find it easier to talk or to listen? Why?

9. When you're alone with God, do you find it easier to talk or to listen? Why?

10. Do you ever intentionally surround yourself with noise? When? Why? What are you trying to accomplish in doing so?

Read the following verses from the Old Testament:

Then Moses and the priests, who are Levites, said to all Israel, "Be silent, O Israel, and listen!"

Deuteronomy 27:9

When you are on your beds, search your hearts and be silent.

Psalm 4:4

But the LORD is in his holy temple; let all the earth be silent before him.

Habakkuk 2:20

11. Based on the above verses, what are some of the circumstances in which we see God wanting his people to be silent? Why do you think God would want people to be silent in those circumstances?

12. What voices that you hear every day are most interesting or intriguing to you? Where does God's voice fit in?

13. Is there a part of you that thinks you already know what God is going to say, so you figure, "What's the point?"

Read the following from 1 Timothy:

I urge, then, first of all, that requests, prayers, intercession and thanksgiving be made for everyone — for kings and all those in authority, that we may live peaceful and quiet lives in all godliness and holiness. This is good, and pleases God our Savior.

1 Timothy 2:1–3

14. What is the connection Paul is making between "peaceful and quiet lives" and "godliness and holiness"?

Read the following from 1 Thessalonians:

Make it your ambition to lead a quiet life, to mind your own business and to work with your hands, just as we told you, so that your daily life may win the respect of outsiders and so that you will not be dependent on anybody.

1 Thessalonians 4:11–12

15. Why does Paul tell the people of the church in Thessalonica to make it their "ambition to lead a quiet life"? What do these words say to you today?

Read the following words of Jesus from the gospel of Matthew:

"Come to me, all you who are weary and burdened, and I will give you rest."

—

Matthew 11:28

16. How can Jesus give you rest when your life is so full of noise?

17. When there is silence, and you are seeking God, do you expect to hear from him? Do you want to? Are you afraid of what you might hear?

18. Do you ever avoid silence because of what you might hear from God? What does that say about the amount of trust you have in God?

19. Why do you think Jesus often "withdrew to lonely places" (Luke 5:16)? Why couldn't he pray where he was, in the midst of the noise of his life? Can you pray in the midst of the noise in your life?

20. Are you afraid to be alone or do you always need someone around you? Why? If you're afraid to be alone, is it you, or God, whom you don't want to face? Why?

Before Moving On

Everybody pair off, preferably with someone you don't know very well. If there is an odd number, three in a group is fine, but no more. With your partner, find a quiet place away from the others. Sit opposite one another. Get comfortable. Let one person signal for all noise to stop. For 10 minutes, say nothing. Look nowhere but at your partner or yourself. Make no noise. No talking, no laughing, no smiling … no nonverbal communication. Just look at one another. At the end of the 10 minutes, note your reactions. Talk about them with each other, then with the group. Was there relief at the end? Did it seem like more or less than 10 minutes? Was it uncomfortable for you and your partner both? Could you sense discomfort in your partner? What was most awkward about it? Why do you think you reacted as you did? Pray together as a group that each of you will take time daily to be alone, as quiet as possible, and will listen for the still, small voice of God. Pray that each of you will become more comfortable being alone with God, and that each of you will take steps to eliminate some of the noises in your lives. Challenge each other to do just that.

Further Personal Reflection

When was the last time you spent time in utter silence? Are silence and solitude foreign words to you? Have they always been? What happened? What would it take to regain some sense of the importance of these disciplines in your life?

How much noise do you allow into your life? Does all the noise in your life make it harder for you to hear God? Does your schedule, your time, and your life look like the schedule, the time, and the life of someone who genuinely wants to hear the still, small voice of God? If not, what, if anything, will you do about it?

Go into a quiet room. Turn off all distracting noises. Make your space — wherever you are — as silent, both audibly and visually, as possible. Close your eyes and do nothing for fifteen minutes. Listen. Check yourself. Are you uncomfortable at all? What makes you uncomfortable? Are you willing to close your ears to others and open your ears to God?

Kickball | 006

—

If God really cares about us,
why don't we have what we want?

—

Kickball | 006

▬▬

Every good and perfect gift is from above, coming down from the Father of the heavenly lights, who does not change like shifting shadows.

▬▬

James 1:17

We always think we know what's missing from our lives in order to really make us happy, don't we? If only I had that car, or that job, or if only I could lose those 15 pounds, then I'd be happy. Really? How often do we want something only to find out that it wasn't that great after all? Sometimes we ask God for things and if he doesn't deliver right away, we start questioning whether or not God really understands or even cares. Do we really trust God? Do we trust that God is good and sees a bigger picture than we ever could? It's easy to want what's right in front of us, but maybe God knows what's better for us.

In this film, the speaker tells the story of the time he and his family were at the mall, and his son saw a toy that he decided he just had to have. The dad tried to reason with him, telling his son that it wasn't a good toy for him to buy, and why, and yet his son persisted, even implying that maybe his dad didn't love him or else he would get it for him. All the while, the dad knew he had something better in mind for his son — a brand new kickball. The parallel is made between this boy, his wants, and his dad and us, our wants, and God. So often we cry out to God, begging for things we want, and think we need, and yet God doesn't give them to us. We have to trust first of all that God is good and because of his goodness, he knows what's best for us.

If anything strikes you while you watch Kickball | 006, write it down ... or make a note and finish it later ... whatever comes to your mind ... just get it on paper ... and then when the time comes, talk about it ...

Talk about Kickball | 006

"We were noticing those kiosks. Have you seen these before? 'Cause there isn't enough stuff for sale at the mall so there have to be these kiosks on wheels where they can sell more stuff."

1. Does our world need more stuff to buy?

"But my son, he stands there, and he says, 'I want one.'"

2. How many things do you see each day that you want?

"I'm like, 'No, no, no. We're leaving, we're going.' And he's like, 'But I want one.'"

3. Is "no" a hard word for you to accept?

"I mean, every boy needs a kickball, right? And so earlier that day, we had decided, you know, after we leave the mall, let's go across the street to the sporting goods store and let's get the boys a kickball."

4. Do you like someone else deciding what you need?

"He looks up at what to him is this massive wall of toys, and he says, 'But I need it!'"

5. Do you ever scream to God about something you "need"?

"So I started laying out my case. 'Like, you don't understand. It's gonna get wrapped around your wrist. It's not gonna work. It's gonna break. It's gonna fly. It's gonna hit you. It's not gonna ...' And he just looks at me with this look. Maybe you've seen this before. He looks at me with this look like, 'But I thought you said you loved me.'"

6. Do you sometimes pout when God says, "No"?

"So I have to walk all the way back, and under great protest, I have to pick him up and carry him back to the car."

7. Who picks you up when you don't get what you want?

"So we take our son up to the wall of kickballs, and he stands there, and he looks up, and with great joy, I say to him, 'Take your pick.'"

8. Do you find joy in giving gifts to others?

"But the point isn't the kickball, is it? I mean, what if, like, what if that was my goal for my kids? That they had more things and better things. That's not the point. More stuff."

9. Is getting more and better things ever the point of your life?

"No, the joy for me, the point for me, is in my relationship with my boys. It's in our interactions, in our connection. The joy for me is when we talk about the things that matter to us."

10. Do you find joy in your relationships with other people?

"So my kids? They ask me for stuff all the time, and I love to give them what they want, but I don't always. Sometimes, I say, 'No.'"

11. Do you ask God for a lot?

"It's because their perspective is limited. There's stuff they don't see that I see. There's stuff they're unaware of."

12. Is your perspective on life limited?

"I mean, what if they actually got everything they asked for right when they asked for it?"

13. Would you want to get everything you asked for right when you asked for it?

"Sometimes they give me this 'I thought you loved me' look, and I'm left saying, 'Well, you just, you got to ... you got to trust me on this.'"

14. Have you ever had to tell someone that they just had to trust you about a certain thing?

"Sometimes we ask God for things, and then when we don't get them, and God doesn't deliver, we think that there must be something wrong with God."

15. Have you ever felt like something was wrong with God when he didn't deliver what you requested?

"Or maybe you've been asking God for something for a while, and you still don't have it. And your question is like, 'How long? How long do I have to wait for this? When is God gonna deliver?'"

16. Do you get frustrated waiting for God to give you what you want?

"And maybe God's perspective is, 'How long? How long till you see that there's a bigger perspective here?'"

17. Do you see your life as part of a larger story that God is authoring?

"Or maybe you're like me. Sometimes you have this sense of, 'God, if you just give me this, then I'd be okay. Then my life would be okay.'"

18. Have you ever prayed believing that if God only gave you what you asked for, you'd be content?

"Or maybe you have this sense of, 'God, if you just give me this, then I'd be happy.' And maybe God's like, 'No. You wouldn't be happy.'"

19. Do you believe God when he tells you that your request won't really make you happy?

"We often have our own ideas of what would be better, don't we? And so we expect God to agree with our idea of what would be better, but God's idea of better is better, isn't it?"

20. Do you believe God's idea of better is better?

"I don't know why there's so much pain and confusion in life, and I don't know how God can stand it, but I do know the question is, 'Do I believe that God is good?' I mean, do you, deep in your bones? What do you really believe God is like? Because until we each deal with this question, then nothing is ever gonna make any sense, is it?"

"Which of you, if his son asks for bread, will give him a stone? Or if he asks for a fish, will give him a snake? If you, then, though you are evil, know how to give good gifts to your children, how much more will your Father in heaven give good gifts to those who ask him!"

Matthew 7:9–11

"So when you find yourself standing at the kiosk, asking, 'Why can't I have what I want?' may you believe that God is good, and that across the street, he has something better."

Kickball | 006 is finished. Now it's your turn. Go back, reread some of the quotes from the film, and discuss the questions raised by those quotes. Then, when you're ready, if there's time, move on to the following questions for more in-depth discussion.

Go a Little Deeper

1. Do you think it brings joy to God to give you good gifts? Why or why not? Has God ever surprised you by saying "No" to something you thought you wanted, only to say "Yes" to something that turned out to be so much better? Discuss.

2. Do you think God delights in saying "No" to you? Why or why not? Regardless of your answer, what circumstances in your life have led you to believe that way?

3. What missing things in your life do you think you need to make your life okay, or happy? How would they make your life okay or happy? Or would they? Why or why not?

4. Do you think God is holding out on you now in some way? In what way? Why do you think he's doing so?

5. Has there been a time in your life when you wanted something so badly that you thought your happiness depended on it — and then you got it? What happened? How long did the "happiness" last? What did you learn from that experience?

6. Has there been a time in your life that you wanted something so badly, only to not get it? How did you react? Did you blame or get mad at God? Did you blame someone else? What did you learn from that experience? Do you still want that "something"?

7. Have you ever demanded an explanation from God when you didn't get something you wanted? Does God owe you an explanation? Why or why not? Do you ever get one, or at least some sense of why God might have said "No"? Does that satisfy you? Do you have a right to question God?

8. Have you ever taken personal responsibility for not getting what you want? Do you believe if you are good enough, or perform a certain way, God will give you what you want? What's the danger in this type of thinking? Does God give to us based on our performance?

9. Do you believe deep down that God is good? Why or why not? What is your answer based on? If not, what would it take for you to believe that God is truly good?

10. How would your life look different if you truly believed that God is good and knows and wants what is best for you? Would it make a difference in the way you looked at life? In the way you lived your life? How?

11. How would admitting that you have a limited perspective, and that God sees infinitely more than you ever can, change the way you live and look at things?

12. Do you ever believe that God's gifts to you come with strings attached? What are those strings? What do you think God expects in return for the good things he gives you?

13. How does your trust in God have any bearing on whether you want certain things for yourself? Can you trust that God is good and yet still want things that God might not want for you? Discuss.

Read the following words of Jesus from the gospel of Matthew:

"Ask and it will be given to you; seek and you will find; knock and the door will be opened to you. For everyone who asks receives; he who seeks finds; and to him who knocks, the door will be opened."

Matthew 7:7–8

14. How do you reconcile Jesus' promise that if you ask, it will be given to you, with the reality that we don't always get what we ask for? What's Jesus getting at here? Why does it sometimes seem like more often than not, you don't get what you ask for?

Read the following from 1 Timothy:

Command those who are rich in this present world not to be arrogant nor to put their hope in wealth, which is so uncertain, but to put their hope in God, who richly provides us with everything for our enjoyment.

1 Timothy 6:17

15. What does Paul mean when he says that God "richly provides us with everything for our enjoyment"? How do you reconcile that with the fact that so often you don't get the things you want for your enjoyment?

Read the following from Jeremiah:

"For I know the plans I have for you," declares the LORD, "plans to prosper you and not to harm you, plans to give you hope and a future. Then you will call upon me and come and pray to me, and I will listen to you. You will seek me and find me when you seek me with all your heart."

Jeremiah 29:11–13

16. How do "hope and a future" compare to the things that you usually want from God? How does this passage illustrate what God wants for his people?

17. Our culture tells us constantly that we need to acquire as much stuff as we can possibly acquire in life. How do we reconcile this message with the message that God is good and therefore, we need to trust him when we don't get what we want? Is Christianity irrelevant in this way? Or is culture? Discuss.

18. Many times we see preachers on television preaching the message that if you ask for something, and you don't get it, then your lack of faith is the problem. What would you say to that? Does such a message lead someone to want to become a follower of Jesus? Why or why not?

19. Has there ever been a time in your life that you have turned away from God because he didn't give you what you wanted? Discuss. What brought you back? Are you back? If not, why not?

Before Moving On

Go around the room and give people an opportunity to name one thing they have been hoping for or asking God for recently. It should be something that deep inside they want very badly for themselves. Ask them to write that thing down on a piece of paper that no one else will see. Tell them to gather in a circle and place their paper in front of them. Pray that all would trust God enough to be able to let go of that desire if that's not something God wants for their lives. At the end of the prayer, ask people to symbolically let go of their "need" for whatever they are wanting by ripping up the piece of paper and throwing it away. Challenge one another to live out their weeks with a belief that God is good, and that he knows what is best for them. Challenge each other to be content knowing that we will not always get what we want, but that we will get what God knows we need.

Further Personal Reflection

Have you ever looked at God as a kind of cosmic Santa Claus, who is just there to give you good gifts? Are you willing to let go of this image of God? What would it take for you to stop expecting God to give you whatever you want?

Do you really, deep down, trust that God is good? What would it take for you to truly believe that God is good and wants what is best for you? Make a list of the things you currently want in life. Break them down into two categories — those things you want for yourself, and those things you want for others. Try to discern the difference between those things you want for yourself that are truly needs and those that are simply wants. Pray that God would help you let go of your wants enough to trust him even if you never get them.

What about your relationship with your own parents or primary caretakers while you were growing up has affected the way you look at God and his goodness to you? Did you get whatever you wanted growing up? Did you grow up lacking things you needed? Did you grow up with a healthy balance? Are you willing to see God for who he is and not as an extension of who your own parents were/are?

Luggage | 007

—

Why is it sometimes so hard to forgive?

—

Luggage | 007

—

"Do not judge, and you will not be judged. Do not condemn, and you will not be condemned. Forgive, and you will be forgiven."

—

Luke 6:37

Maybe a friend turned their back on you. Maybe someone you loved betrayed you. We all have wounds and we end up carrying around these things that people have done to us for weeks, months, and sometimes even years. It isn't always easy to forgive these people and after a while these hurts can get really heavy. So the only way to feel better seems to be somehow getting back at the people that hurt us, to get revenge. But does revenge ever truly satisfy? Maybe forgiving isn't something you do for someone else to let them off the hook. Maybe forgiveness is about you. God didn't create you to carry these wounds around. God created you to be free.

In this film, the speaker talks about how we so often react to wrongs others do to us. All too often, we want to get revenge on the other person. The speaker challenges that desire for revenge, asking us if that might mean we really don't trust God to sort things out. He contrasts this with what Jesus teaches: that we are to forgive, as God has forgiven us. In doing so, we may find that we are able to be freer from the pain that weighs us down so much.

If anything strikes you while you watch Luggage | 007, write it down … or make a note and finish it later … whatever comes to your mind … just get it on paper … and then when the time comes, talk about it …

Talk about Luggage | 007

"And he's trying to kind of convince himself that it's gonna be okay, but it doesn't look like she is coming back."

1. Do you need to let go of someone?

"It's like everyone I know has wounds, and some are small, kind of petty, like, 'You know what, you just need to get over it.' But for a lot of people ... they're big, and serious, and deep wounds."

2. Do you have deep wounds?

"It's like we could speculate why all this happens, and why people do these kinds of things, and we could try to figure it out forever, but I think what we want, what we want is to be free from this, don't we? We want to be alive and healthy and whole."

3. Does being alive and healthy and whole sound appealing to you?

"I mean, I don't want what somebody else did to me to determine what my life is gonna be like, do you?"

4. Do you let the wounds other people gave you determine how your life is going to be?

"It's like you try not to think about it, but then if you're like me, then you end up thinking about it more than ever, and it's like we want to put this stuff behind us. But how?"

5. Are you dwelling on past hurts?

"Or have you ever had this happen? It's like you think you're over it, you think you're okay, you think it's in the past and then you either run into the person or you run into something that reminds you of them and what they did to you, and then it all comes back like worse than ever, and it's like you thought you were over it, but now you're more into it than ever, and the wound is, like, reopened, and it hurts more than ever. And then it becomes a day, or a week or ten years later, and now it's become like a part of you."

6. Has a past wound become a part of who you are?

"Then eventually what happens is revenge becomes our only hope, and we aren't free."

7. Does revenge feel good?

"Where was God when this happened to me?"

8. Have you ever asked, "Where was God when this happened to me?"

He rules forever by his power, his eyes watch the nations — let not the rebellious rise up against him.
___
Psalm 66:7

The eyes of the LORD are everywhere, keeping watch on the wicked and the good.
___
Proverbs 15:3

"So whatever was done to you, whatever wrong was done to any of us, God saw it. It's like God was right there."

9. Do you believe God sees you when you are hurt by another person?

Do not take revenge, my friends, but leave room for God's wrath, for it is written: "It is mine to avenge; I will repay," says the Lord.

—

Romans 12:19

"It's like the writer says, 'Just turn it over to God. Let God take care of it.' Which is, it's like a nice idea, but it isn't very easy to do, is it?"

10. Is it easy for you to let go and let God sort it out when it comes to the times people have hurt you?

"It's 'cause, like, revenge … revenge is like part of our world, isn't it? I mean, we talk like this all the time."

"Think about revenge, like, at the deepest spiritual levels. I mean, revenge is really saying to God, 'God, I don't trust you to deal with this situation. This person wronged me, and I can't turn it over to you, because I don't know what you're gonna do here.' And so revenge is like saying, 'God, not only don't I trust you, but if I get revenge, then I can determine what happens here. I can control the situation.' And so revenge is like saying to God, 'I don't trust you. I actually think I can do your job better than you can.'"

11. Do you like to try to control your world?

"Revenge doesn't satisfy, does it? I mean, have you ever really evened the score? I mean, have you ever really gotten revenge and then felt good about yourself? It's because revenge doesn't work, does it?"

"I think this is why freedom is so central to Jesus' teachings. It's, like, right at the heart of his message is this simple claim that God has forgiven us of all of our sins, doesn't hold any of our past against us. 'Cause none of us have clean hands, do we? I mean, we've all wronged someone. But with Jesus, there is no condemnation. There is no list of wrongs. There is no judgment. It's like the cross is God's way of saying, 'I don't hold your past against you.'"

12. Do you see the cross as God's way of saying, "I don't hold your past against you"?

"Some people have a warped view of God; that God's, like, waiting, to just, like, punish them for any wrong thing they do."

13. Do you see God as just waiting to punish you when you do something wrong?

"So even when it comes to doing the right thing, like in this case, forgiveness, there is this paranoia that if they step out of line at all, God's like, waiting right there to squash them."

14. Do you live in constant fear of God's judgment?

"Anything bad that happens, people assume is like God punishing them 'cause they weren't doing the right thing at that time or that everything is some sort of judgment or punishment."

15. Do you view misfortune in your life as some sort of judgment or punishment?

"But this isn't the kind of picture that Jesus paints of God. Jesus gives us these pictures of a God who is, like, full of love and grace and mercy and forgiveness, who, like, keeps pursuing us and who keeps insisting that his way is the best possible way to live. So when I forgive somebody, I am giving them what God has given to me."

16. Have you experienced God's forgiveness?

"Have you ever heard somebody say that, like, because of something that was done to them, they've been, like, 'You know what? You don't understand. What they did to me is so horrible, I will never forgive them. I can't forgive them for what they did.' But, like, what if God said that?"

"It's like some people are destructive, and they're toxic, and they're gonna wrong us, and they're gonna do it over and over again, and the relationship may never go back to how it was. And so with some people, we might need to set up boundaries with them, put some space. Some people, we may not even be able to be around them. Because forgiving isn't always forgetting."

17. Do you see forgiving as forgetting?

"And so to forgive is to let it go, is to set them free, is to give up on the desire for revenge, but ultimately, to really forgive somebody, I have to actually wish them well. I have to hope that good comes their way, 'cause if I'm still unable to wish them well and wish them good, then I'm really just waiting for them to get punished, and I really … I haven't forgiven them."

18. Can you wish someone well who has hurt you deeply?

"Maybe the real point of forgiveness isn't other people. I mean, we talk about setting them free and letting it go, but maybe forgiveness is ultimately about me and about you, it's about us. Because when I forgive somebody, and I set them free, it's like I'm really setting myself free. It's like when I forgive them, and I let them off the hook, I'm really letting myself off the hook."

19. Do you need to let yourself off the hook by forgiving someone?

"God didn't create you to carry that stuff around. God created you to be free, like, free from bitterness, free from rage, and anger, and revenge. Free from feeling like you're the judge of the world."

20. Do you ever feel like you're the judge of the world?

"May you forgive as you've been forgiven. May you give to others what's been given to you. May you set someone free and find out that it was you. And may you do it today, because you might not have the chance tomorrow."

Luggage | 007 is finished. Now it's your turn. Go back, reread some of the quotes from the film, and discuss the questions raised by those quotes. Then, when you're ready, if there's time, move on to the following questions for more in-depth discussion.

Go a Little Deeper

1. How have your wounds helped to shape the person you are today?

2. The speaker asks the question, What if God had the same view of forgiveness as you do, and he refused to forgive you for what you've done? Where would that leave you? Do you want to serve an unforgiving God, a God who punished you for every wrong thing you do? Why or why not?

3. Did you grow up in a home that was more concerned with punishment and revenge than with forgiveness, mercy, and grace? How does your relationship with your parents growing up affect the way you see revenge and forgiveness? How do these views affect the way you treat others who have wronged you?

4. When was the last time you sought revenge against someone who hurt or betrayed you? Did you get it? How did it feel? Did it satisfy this person's debt against you? Do you still want revenge?

5. When was the last time you truly forgave someone? How did that feel? Did you feel like you were somehow being cheated? If so, have you truly forgiven them? Why or why not?

6. Have you ever had to forgive someone, yet also walk away from them? How difficult or easy was that? What happened?

7. If, as the speaker says, God was right there when you were wronged, why do you think he didn't step in to stop it from happening? Does that make you angry? Do you blame God for the hurts other people have done to you?

8. How do you react when someone forgives you? Are you able to accept their forgiveness, or do you always look for the strings that might be attached? Do you feel like you need to somehow make up for the wrongs you have done to them?

9. How do you react to God's forgiveness? Are you able to accept God's forgiveness, or do you look for strings? Do you feel like you need to somehow make up to God for the wrongs you have done? How can you make them up to God? Will your attempts to make them up to him satisfy him? How can God ever be satisfied with you?

10. Do you need to be forgiven by God? Why or why not?

Read the following verse from Romans:

For all have sinned and fall short of the glory of God.

⸺

Romans 3:23

11. What does it mean to sin and fall short of the glory of God? Do you accept that you have sinned and fall short of the glory of God? Is this a difficult thing for you to admit? Why or why not? In light of this, do you need to be forgiven by God?

12. What does it mean when it says that "the wages of sin is death"? Do you deserve to die for your sins? Do you believe deep down that you have done too much wrong to be truly forgiven by God? Do you want to be forgiven by God?

13. How does one receive forgiveness from God? What about those who reject God's free gift of forgiveness?

Read the following from Hebrews:

Nothing in all creation is hidden from God's sight. Everything is uncovered and laid bare before the eyes of him to whom we must give account.

Hebrews 4:13

14. How does it make you feel to know that God sees everything you do? Do you want to give an account to God? What would your account look like?

15. What does it mean when it says that Jesus was tempted in every way, but was without sin? What does that mean for your life, and for mine? What does it mean when it says we can "approach the throne of grace with confidence?" In light of that, would you be confident to stand before God and account for your life? Why or why not?

Read the following from Romans:

Bless those who persecute you; bless and do not curse. Rejoice with those who rejoice; mourn with those who mourn. Live in harmony with one another. Do not be proud, but be willing to associate with people of low position. Do not be conceited. Do not repay anyone evil for evil.

Romans 12:14–17

16. Is it easy for you to do what these verses say, especially as they talk about not repaying evil for evil, not taking revenge, overcoming evil with good? Why or why not?

17. Is it risky to forgive someone the way God wants you to? What would it cost you?

Read the following from Hebrews:

But we see Jesus, who was made a little lower than the angels, now crowned with glory and honor because he suffered death, so that by the grace of God he might taste death for everyone.

Hebrews 2:9

18. What did it cost God to forgive you?

Before Moving On

Go around the room and give people an opportunity to think of one person (do not share the name of the person) in their lives that they need to forgive. If they care to share how that person wronged them, that's fine. If not, that's okay too. Ask them to write the name of the person on a piece of paper that no one else will see. Tell them to gather in a circle and hold the paper with the person's name in their hands. Pray that all would trust God enough to be able to let go of that pain and to forgive that person. Ask each person to pray, "Lord, help me to forgive the one whose name I've written down." At the end of the prayer, challenge each other to seek out that person in the coming days and to forgive them. Challenge them to trust God enough to mean it and to see what a difference it makes in their own lives when they do so.

Ask if there is anyone in the group who has not yet experienced God's forgiveness, but would like to. Encourage them to stay after the rest of the group leaves. Pray for them and with them, that they would accept God's provision for their sin, his Son, Jesus.

Further Personal Reflection

Think of your deepest wound. Sit down and write about it. How did someone wrong you? Have you forgiven them? How has holding onto that pain hurt you even further? What would it take for you to forgive them? What would that do to your pain? If that person died before you had a chance to make amends with them, what kind of regrets would you have? If that person has already died, what regrets do you have?

Do you have any past hurts for which you are still blaming God? Do you need to let them go? Pray that God would help you do so.

What would it take for you to become the type of person Jesus describes here? Are you willing to ask God to help you become that kind of person? Why or why not?

Dust | 008

—

What does God see in us?

Dust | 008

—

"I will give you the keys of the kingdom of heaven; whatever you bind on earth will be bound in heaven, and whatever you loose on earth will be loosed in heaven."

—

Matthew 16:19

Believing in God is important, but what about God believing in us? Believing that we can actually be the kind of people we were meant to be. People of love, compassion, peace, forgiveness, and hope. People who try to do the right thing all of the time. Who act on the endless opportunities around us every day for good, beauty, and truth. It's easy for us to sometimes get down on ourselves. To feel "not good enough" or feel like we don't have what it takes. But maybe if we had more insight into the culture that Jesus grew up in and some of the radical things he did, we'd understand the faith that God has in all of us.

In this film, the speaker discusses the relationship in biblical times between a rabbi and his disciples. He talks about how Jesus chose people to follow him who had not made the cut with other rabbis … people who were not exactly the cream of the crop. Yet, as we look at history, we see that Jesus' disciples literally changed the world. The speaker goes on to discuss what that reality might mean for us, who are often so riddled with self-doubt that we don't believe we can do anything significant for God.

If anything strikes you while you watch Dust | 008, write it down … or make a note and finish it later … whatever comes to your mind … just get it on paper … and then when the time comes, talk about it …

Talk about Dust | 008

"I want to be the kind of person who does the right thing. And I don't just mean the big things where right and wrong are obvious and easy, but I mean the small things, the subtle, unnoticed things."

1. Do you want to be the kind of person who does the right thing?

"You know, what I do when no one's watching."

2. What do you do when no one is watching?

"Because it's so easy to let those small things slip away. And it's those endless choices that we make every day that shape us into the kinds of people that we are."

3. Do you believe you're shaped by the small choices you make?

Immediately Jesus made the disciples get into the boat and go on ahead of him to the other side, while he dismissed the crowd. After he had dismissed them, he went up on a mountainside by himself to pray. When evening came, he was there alone, but the boat was already a considerable distance from land, buffeted by the waves because the wind was against it. During the fourth watch of the night Jesus went out to them, walking on the lake. When the disciples saw him walking on the lake, they were terrified. "It's a ghost," they said, and cried out in fear. But Jesus immediately said to them: "Take courage! It is I. Don't be afraid." "Lord, if it's you," Peter replied, "tell me to come to you on the water." "Come," he said. Then Peter got down out of the boat, walked on the water and came toward Jesus. But when he saw the wind, he was afraid and, beginning to sink, cried out, "Lord, save me!" Immediately Jesus reached out his hand and caught him. "You of little faith," he said, "why did you doubt?"

▬

Matthew 14:22–31

"But a disciple is something far deeper. A disciple just doesn't want to know what the rabbi knows. A disciple wants to be like the rabbi and wants to learn to do what the rabbi does."

4. Who do you emulate?

"They knew exactly what it meant to be covered in the dust of your rabbi."

5. Whose dust covers you?

"In the Bible around the age of 30 we have Jesus walking down the shore along the Sea of Galilee, and he comes across Peter, and Andrew, and they're fishermen. And Jesus says to them, 'Come. Follow me.' Well, if they're fishermen, and Jesus calls them to be his disciples, then they're not following another rabbi, and if they're not following another rabbi, they're not the best of the best. They didn't make the cut."

6. Do you think of Jesus' disciples as ones who didn't make the cut?

"Rabbis were the most honored, respected, revered people anywhere. I mean, the best of the best of the best were the only ones who got to be rabbis. And this rabbi comes down the beach and says to you, 'Come. Follow me.' What's he really saying? What he's really saying is, 'I think you could do what I do.' He's saying, 'You can be like me.' Of course you'd drop your nets and follow him."

7. Would you have dropped everything to follow Jesus?

"Jesus chooses them 'cause his movement is for everybody. It's for rich and for poor, and for women and men, and educated and uneducated."

"It's for the peasants and the scholars. It's like a movement of anybodies, and he calls them — the JV, the B team, the not-good-enoughs — he calls them to be his disciples and they change the course of human history."

8. Does it surprise you to think of a bunch of "anybodies" changing the course of human history?

"Why is Peter's first reaction, 'If it's you, then tell me to come to you'? Because he's a disciple, he's oriented his whole life, devoted his whole life, to doing what he sees his rabbi doing. Learning to be like his rabbi. So, he sees his rabbi walking on water, and what's the first thing he wants to do? 'I want to walk on water too. I want to be like my rabbi.'"

9. Do you want to be like Jesus?

"The text reads that Jesus immediately caught him and said, 'You of little faith, why did you doubt?'"

10. Do you often doubt?

"Now, I always assumed that Peter doubts Jesus. But Jesus isn't sinking! Who does Peter doubt? He doubts himself. He loses faith in himself that he can actually be like his rabbi. Jesus wouldn't have called him if he didn't think he could be like him. Jesus even reminds his disciples of this at one point. He says to them, 'Wait, wait, wait, you didn't choose me. I chose you.'"

11. Has Jesus chosen you to follow him?

"The rabbi doesn't choose you unless the rabbi thinks that you can do what he does, that you can be like him. All my life I've heard people talk about believing in God. But God believes in us. In you. In me. I mean, faith in Jesus is important, but what about Jesus' faith in us? I mean, he must have faith in us, because he leaves it all in the hands of these disciples. What's the last thing Jesus says to them? He says to them, 'Now you go and make more disciples.' He leaves it all in the hands of these anybodies, and they do it! What if we can actually be the kinds of people that God created us to be?"

12. Do you want to live as God created you to live?

"What if he actually believes that we can be the kind of people who live like Jesus lived? And the kinds of people who take action because we're aware of all of these endless opportunities around us all the time for good, for beauty, for truth. I mean, Jesus has faith that you can follow him and you can be like him. He believes it."

13. Do you see yourself as one who can be like Jesus?

"May you believe in God. But may you come to see that God believes in you. May you have faith in Jesus. But may you come to see that Jesus has faith that you can be like him. A person of love and compassion and truth, a person of forgiveness and peace and grace and joy and hope. And may you be covered in the dust of your rabbi, Jesus."

Dust | 008 is finished. Now it's your turn. Go back, reread some of the quotes from the film, and discuss the questions raised by those quotes. Then, when you're ready, if there's time, move on to the following questions for more in-depth discussion.

Go a Little Deeper

1. Do you find it easy to do the right thing when it will go virtually unnoticed? Why or why not?

2. Do you think it's important to do the right thing when no one is looking? Why or why not? Do you ever think that no one is really noticing what you do? Does God notice? Does he count?

3. Have you ever thought about Jesus as your rabbi? Would you consider yourself a disciple of Jesus? How would seeing yourself as Jesus' disciple affect the way you live and see life?

4. When the speaker says that Jesus' disciples wouldn't have been considered the best of the best, how does that strike you? What implications are there for you and me today? Discuss.

Read the following from 1 Corinthians:

Brothers, think of what you were when you were called. Not many of you were wise by human standards; not many were influential; not many were of noble birth. But God chose the foolish things of the world to shame the wise; God chose the weak things of the world to shame the strong. He chose the lowly things of this world and the despised things — and the things that are not — to nullify the things that are, so that no one may boast before him.

▬

1 Corinthians 1:26–29

5. What does it mean when it says that God chose the foolish things of the world to shame the wise? Do you see yourself as one of the foolish things of the world? One of the weak? One of the lowly? Why or why not?

6. What do you think it means when it says "so that no one may boast before him"?

7. Did you grow up believing that Christianity was for the elite or for the anybodies? Why? What do you believe now? Why? What's the truth?

8. The speaker asserts that Jesus' bunch of anybodies changed the course of human history. In what ways did they change the course of human history? How would the world be different if they hadn't followed Jesus?

9. In what ways are followers of Christ impacting the world today? Do you think Christians are having the impact they could have? Do you think disciples of Jesus are still changing the course of human history today? Why or why not? What, if anything, is missing?

10. Do you doubt yourself? Do you ever feel insecure, or insignificant? Why or why not?

11. Do your self-doubts affect your faith? In what way? How do they affect the way you live?

12. Have you ever let self-doubt prevent you from doing something you know God wanted you to do? Talk about it.

Read the following from Philippians:

I can do everything through him who gives me strength.

—

Philippians 4:13

13. Do you believe that you can do everything through Jesus? What does that mean to you? How much room is there for insecurity or doubt in light of this? Discuss.

14. The speaker says that God believes in you. Does that make you uncomfortable? Why or why not? Does it make you uncomfortable when he says that Jesus has faith in you? Why or why not?

15. What does God believe about you?

Read the following from the gospel of John:

"I tell you the truth, anyone who has faith in me will do what I have been doing. He will do even greater things than these, because I am going to the Father."

—

John 14:12

16. What does Jesus believe about his disciples?

Read the following from the gospel of John:

"If you love me, you will obey what I command. And I will ask the Father, and he will give you another Counselor to be with you forever."

——

John 14:15

"All this I have spoken while still with you. But the Counselor, the Holy Spirit, whom the Father will send in my name, will teach you all things and will remind you of everything I have said to you."

——

John 14:25–26

17. Based on these verses, how does Jesus see the Holy Spirit's role in the disciples' lives? How might the Holy Spirit help Jesus' disciples live more like him?

Read the following from Galatians:

So I say, live by the Spirit, and you will not gratify the desires of the sinful nature. For the sinful nature desires what is contrary to the Spirit, and the Spirit what is contrary to the sinful nature. They are in conflict with each other, so that you do not do what you want. But if you are led by the Spirit, you are not under law. The acts of the sinful nature are obvious: sexual immorality, impurity and debauchery; idolatry and witchcraft; hatred, discord, jealousy, fits of rage, selfish ambition, dissensions, factions and envy; drunkenness, orgies, and the like. I warn you, as I did before, that those who live like this will not inherit the kingdom of God. But the fruit of the Spirit is love, joy, peace, patience, kindness, goodness, faithfulness, gentleness and self-control. Against such things there is no law.

——

Galatians 5:16–23

18. Based on these verses, what difference does the Holy Spirit make in the lives of followers of Jesus? Does your life look like that? In what way?

Before Moving On

Go around the room and ask everybody to pair up. Have each person share with their partner one thing they would do for God if they had more faith. Encourage people to dream big. Challenge each other to examine what they want to do, and if it's something that they believe God would want them to do, then they should do whatever it takes, not letting their own self-doubt hold them back. Pray for one another — that each of you will have boldness to step out in faith and live your lives like Jesus lived his and wants you to live yours.

Further Personal Reflection

Think of someone in your life whom you wanted to emulate when you were younger. What was it about them that made you want to be like them? How would your life look if you had never known them?

Look in the mirror. What would it take for you to see yourself as Jesus' disciple? How will that make a difference in your life? What would it take for you to not only see him as your Savior, but to try to emulate him in your life?

How would the world be different if you lived more like Jesus? Would there be any difference? What can God do through you?